PIG'S
PLOUGHMAN

MONSTERS OF MYTHOLOGY

25 VOLUMES

Hellenic

Amycus
Anteus
The Calydonian Boar
Cerberus
Chimaera
The Cyclopes
The Dragon of Boeotia
The Furies
Geryon
Harpalyce
Hecate
The Hydra
Ladon
Medusa
The Minotaur
The Nemean Lion
Procrustes
Scylla and Charybdis
The Sirens
The Spear-birds
The Sphinx

Norse

Fafnir
Fenris

Celtic

Drabne of Dole
Pig's Ploughman

MONSTERS OF MYTHOLOGY

PIG'S PLOUGHMAN

Bernard Evslin

CHELSEA HOUSE PUBLISHERS

New York   Philadelphia

1990

EDITOR
Remmel Nunn

ART DIRECTOR
Maria Epes

PICTURE RESEARCHER
Susan Quist

SENIOR DESIGNER
Marjorie Zaum

EDITORIAL ASSISTANTS
Seeta Chaganti, Nate Eaton, Mark Rifkin

3   5   7   9   8   6   4   2

Library of Congress Cataloging-in-Publication Data

Evslin, Bernard.
Pig's Ploughman / Bernard Evslin.

p.   cm.—(Monsters of mythology)

Summary: Recounts the myth of Vilemurk, or the Pig's Ploughman, the
murderous Hog Who Ate the Sun who battles the hero Finn McCool in
the ancient land of Eire.
ISBN 1-55546-256-1
1. Vilemurk (Celtic mythology)—Juvenile literature. 2. Finn
MacCumhaill, 3rd cent.—Juvenile literature. [1. Vilemurk (Celtic
mythology) 2. Finn MacCool. 3. Mythology, Celtic.] I. Title.
II. Series: Evslin, Bernard. Monsters of mythology.
BL915.V54E97   1990   398.2′09415—dc20
89-34592   CIP   AC

Printed in Mexico

A full turn of the wheel
brings back GALEAL—
a more ardent reader than ever

Characters

Monsters

Pig's Ploughman	The Lord of Winter, also known as Vilemurk
Dragon	Ice-breathing monster who serves Vilemurk
Mist crones	Winter demons
Head smith	A mountain troll

Gods

Lyr	God of the Sea who doubles as a monster according to mood

Mortals

Finn McCool	A young hero
Houlihan	Slovenly cattle breeder and thief
Kathleen	Houlihan's daughter

Carth of the Cove	Kathleen's husband
Widow of the Cove	Kathleen's mother-in-law

Animals

Cat	A huge black tom, Finn's loyal friend
Hawk	A falcon, another loyal friend of Finn's
Seven sharks	
Three swans	

Contents

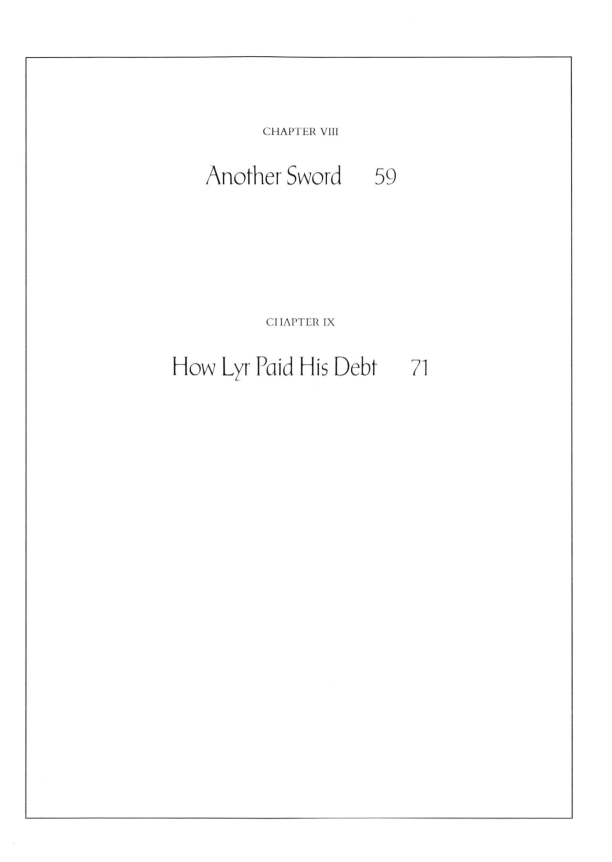

PIG'S
PLOUGHMAN

Names for the Frost Fiend

Only the Irish know that Noah had four sons, not three, as the Bible claims. The youngest son was a hellion and a wag. He jeered at his father's weather forecasts and made unkind remarks about the big, clumsy boat the old man was building. Noah lost his temper and took off after him with an axe, and the lad decided it might be wiser to leave home. But he must have learned something from his father because, when the Flood began, he was ready with a tiny ark of his own in which he stowed his young bride, two pigs and two potatoes, and announced that he would sail far, far to the west beyond people and beyond sin. He landed on an island now called Eire.

The people of this island were so used to rain that they had even managed to live through the Flood, although, it is said, some of them never quite dried out, even to this day. But after the heavy rain had stopped falling the sky was still covered by clouds, and these clouds pressed low, shrouding the land in thick fog.

The people were frightened. They were used to fog also, but this was too thick, and was lasting too long. Fear spawned rumor—which ran wild and clotted into tales. Folk whispered

Vilemurk—it was said—the Lord of Winter, the Frost Fiend,
had turned himself into a gigantic hog and eaten
the sun the way a pig eats an apple.

dreadful things to each other about the rampaging weather gods, who were more like demons, but who were the only gods they knew. Vilemurk—it was said—the Lord of Winter, the Frost Fiend, had turned himself into a gigantic hog and eaten the sun the way a pig eats an apple.

One night a strong wind blew, scouring the sky, which seemed to have come much closer to earth, or else the island was floating higher because of the flood tide. Whatever the reason, though, the stars were larger and brighter and seemed to have rearranged themselves. Directly overhead burned a pattern of stars in the shape of a plough whose prongs were pointing toward the North Star, grown huge. Behind the plough loomed a great hunched shape, either bear or boar. A cry arose from the terrified folk:

"A starry beast stalks the sky! Why? . . . Why?"

"He is ploughing," said the newcomer, that son of Noah who had come floating in out of the Flood and was already answering questions with easy assurance. "He ploughs the black loam of the sky planting wind-seed, rain-seed . . ."

"Is he bear—or boar?"

"Boar," said the young man, whose name was Meath. "He is the Hog Who Eats the Sun. He is Vilemurk, Lord of Winter."

They believed what he told them. For this slender, burning-eyed young man had somehow guided his small house-shaped boat through the howling, whirling flood. He cast an aura of wizardry and spoke with the authority of one whose family had been chosen for survival by an angry god in a far place.

And since that time, Vilemurk, the Frost Fiend, has been known as the Hog Who Eats the Sun, and has been given a second name—Pig's Ploughman.

Why must we know about this last son of Noah? Because he became known as Cuhal ni Tyrne, or King of the Wave in a tongue ancient beyond knowledge, and his descendants became the great clan Cuhal, of which Finn McCuhal was the last and greatest hero. So it was that young Finn always felt a clan loyalty to Lyr, God of the Sea—a loyalty that was to lead him into the greatest peril of his life.

2

Gods at Odds

ow, from the very beginning of things Vile-murk had hated Lyr because, huff and puff and chill as he would, the Frost Fiend could never quite freeze the wide seas. Even in the coldest winter they would ice up only a short way past the shore. For centuries the two gods had been locked in feud; then, suddenly, the feud flared into open warfare. It came about this way:

One day in early spring, Lyr made one of his rare trips inland to inspect certain rivers that flow to the sea, and are part of his domain. He spied a beautiful ice maiden, dispatched by Vilemurk to delay the spring and blow her icy breath upon streams and ponds that were trying to thaw, and freeze them fast.

Lyr watched the ice maiden for a while, and liked what he saw. He flung his green cloak about her and flew back with her to his crystal and coral island in the very middle of the seven seas. She resisted at first, but he promised her this and that if she would consent to stay with him and become his youngest wife. It meant being a queen, of course, and he offered her the choicest pearls of the oyster crop, and an ivory comb curiously carved, and her own dolphin chariot, and a mermaid's tail for when she wished to travel underwater. So she agreed to stay with him, and became the youngest and most beautiful of all his briny brides.

Vilemurk fell into a fury when he learned that someone had stolen his favorite ice maiden, and that this someone was his old enemy, Lyr. Now, of course, he hated the sea god worse than ever, with a hatred that had to end in death or torment.

For all his fury, though, he made a careful plan. He spread a tale of treasure in the northern sea where Vilemurk holds more power than in other places, and keeps great fleets of ice thronging the open waters, and has dyed all the animals the color of snow. The tale he spread was one meant to appeal to Lyr, lover of all that glitters. A giant crystal, the rumor said, had been spotted floating in the black northern waters. A pure water crystal larger than the largest iceberg, hard as a diamond, and so carved by eons of knife-edged polar winds that it was all polished surfaces and glittering angles. When the sun hit it, the giant crystal blazed forth with rainbow light, making all the jewels of earth seem drabber than pebbles you find in the dust.

Reports of this wondrous crystal fired Lyr with a wild craving, and he rushed off north to see for himself. He went in such haste that he left behind his escort of swordfish and spearfish and fire eels and shark-toothed mermen, and all ignorant and unguarded sped northward to where his enemy, Vilemurk, the murderous Pig's Ploughman, lay in ambush.

Now, Vilemurk had brought with him all the disastrous crew that he commanded . . .

The huge, coiled serpentine monster that lies under earth, stone asleep, until he awakes in rage to make the earth quake.

And the giants who dwell in hollow mountains whose cooking fires are called volcanoes.

And the Master of Winds, who can whistle up a hurricane as a man whistles for his dog.

All these and more: The bat-winged mist hags who, flying low and in formation, can lay a blindness on earth and sea. Those same chill crones whose breath can freeze the marrow. When they have nothing else to do they go about robbing cradles of girl babies and train them up as ice maidens.

All these lay in wait for the God of the Sea. Lyr came flying north, traveling alone in his sky chariot drawn by flying fishes. Toward a rumored treasure and an unknown foe he rushed, standing tall in his chariot, clad in whale-skin armor with a mantle of seal furs swinging from his mighty shoulders, wearing his crown of pearls, white beard flying, holding his three-pronged spear, which he could hurl like a thunderbolt if he wished, or handle as delicately as a seamstress does her needle. Northward he came, flashing across the low horizon, making a strange sun in the northern sky, which was entering its season of night.

All aglitter, hot with greed, Lyr came riding across the sky to seek the huge gem of water crystal he had heard about—and flew right into Vilemurk's ambush.

But young Finn knew nothing of this god-feud that was to trap him in its mighty coils. Nor did he know anything at all about a certain lout named Houlihan, whose notable daughter was to figure so importantly in this adventure.

3

Houlihan's Daughter

The fact of it is—and a fact or two, but not too many, will fit pleasantly into a true story—the fact is that Houlihan's wife, when he had one in the long ago, was altogether too tidy. How Houlihan had come to choose her was a mystery. He was a big, brawling red-pelted man; the only time he bathed was when he was caught in the rain. No member of his family had worn shoes since the beginning of time, nor did he ever use knife at table, but tore meat with his hands, then wiped them on his beard. Yet when it came time to marry he chose this brisk little person who fairly shone with cleanliness, and who shook with fury at the mere shadow of dust. Why did he woo her? Why did she allow herself to be won? There is a puzzle between man and woman beyond ordinary meaning, and time can turn a girl into a hag and a man into a stick and the mystery into a gall, but it is born again at wakes and weddings—which is perhaps why they are so popular.

Anyway, this little wife of Houlihan's took the stinking pen that was his farm and made it sweet as a garden of herbs. By heaven, when she was finished the pigs smelled like violets; there was not a nettle or briar to be seen on the place; her pots hung over the hob like dark suns, and fence and barn were whitewashed so white it hurt the eye to look at them.

She cleaned up her husband, too. Wouldn't let him near her on their wedding night, rumor said, until he had soaked himself in the river for a full hour, scrubbing himself raw while she stood on the bank telling him what to do. And after she had him awhile, why, hair and beard were clipped, and he was combed and curried and scrubbed and rubbed until he was sleek as an otter. And he seemed happy that way, and anyone who dared jest about new ways or new wife felt the weight of his fist, which was the heaviest in that part of Leinster.

But for all her bustle, her ways were never grim. Light-footed she was, and pleasant of voice; built small with sapling grace, she seemed to distill light as she went. Too much, perhaps. For certain *drees* of darkness were deeply offended and resolved to blot her. Of what she most loathed they took the essence and concocted a creature. Out of rot and stench and slime, dead birds, roaches, and rats, they cooked up something that looked like a huge ball of clotted hair, something between a sow and a spider, but ten feet round. And one day in the early spring as she was weeding her garden, it rolled upon her, blotting her light.

Big Red Houlihan was left with a two-month-old daughter and a house and fields shining with memory, and a bewilderment turning into rage, which turned into pure hell-spite.

He killed one or two of his neighbors in the first days of his wrath, but simple murder left him unslaked. He needed to go beyond man in his killing. With mighty blows of his axe he knocked down his house and moved into the barn. He could not sleep, so to fill his nights he went cattle raiding, hoping to be caught and killed after a last bloody brawl. But by prudence or design his neighbors left him strictly alone when he was helping himself to their stock. He herded the stolen cows and pigs in great droves into his barn. Nor did he ever clean that barn, but

*At the very center of this mountain
of filth lived Houlihan.*

lived there with his little daughter in the muck and mire, which
grew more dreadful each day.

Finally, Houlihan's barn had become the biggest midden in
all Eire, an unbelievably putrid heap that stank all his neighbors
out of that part of the country and put a taint upon the air clear
to Ulster. When the wind was right, it was said you could smell
that barn across the Giant's Causeway all the way into Scotland.
And at the very center of this mountain of filth lived Houlihan,
so foul now he could scarcely be distinguished from one of his
dung-splattered bulls. Here too, among the crud–worms and flies

the size of sparrows, grew his daughter, though no one could tell what she looked like, so thick was her mask of dirt.

Now this daughter, whose name was Kathleen, loved her father because he belonged to her, and was even fond of her home, for she knew no other. Nevertheless, as she grew older she grew restless, until one day Houlihan said:

"Now stop your wriggling and squirming, girl. You need a husband to calm you down."

"A husband!" she shrieked. "And who would marry me in my filthy state?"

"Why, whatever lad I catch for you—after I explain his duties a time or two."

"Thank you. I'll catch my own."

"Then be about it, and good luck to you. But be sure you bring him here to live. For I need you to serve me, and he can help."

"Bring him back to this muck and mire? Why should I?"

"Because I tell you to."

"Why should he?"

"You will not find me meddling in those delicate questions that arise between man and bride. I am sure you will be able to put the matter to him persuasively, for you were ever a dutiful girl, and it is I who bid you—I, Red Houlihan, who curses every day that keeps him on this pitiful dung heap of earth, and in the long, deep, blackness of whose life you have been the only light."

"I'm off," she said. "I'll be back with my husband, or perhaps alone."

"One last word," said Houlihan. "Seek you love on the far bank of a river that has no bridge."

"Yes, Father."

Now, on the other side of the river there lived a gentle-man-nered, smiling lad with hair like peach floss. Nineteen years old he was, but he had been kept quite childlike by his mother, who was known as the Widow of the Cove. The lad's name was Carth. What he liked to do best in the world was to lie on a rock in the sun, thinking nothing at all until pictures began drifting through his head. He did not know where they came from or where they were going, but he liked to watch them while they were there. One day the same picture kept swimming in his head: a girl, dripping wet.

Now, as it happened, in his nineteen years he had never seen a girl of any kind, wet or dry. His mother had kept him from all such, fearing that one of the creatures might decide to marry her boy before he was ripe. And this thought threw her into such a rage that she kept him close to his own homestead, and never allowed him to roam.

When he opened his eyes he saw a wet girl
on the riverbank wringing out
her long red hair . . .

So when he saw this wet girl in a waking dream, she made the first he had ever seen, and he doted upon her, saying to himself: "Oh, how happy I would be if she were real. How softly I would welcome her, offering to do her any service—to chop wood and fetch water, and slop her pigs, and milk her cow, and lay a fire in her hearth so that she might dry herself in its warmth, combing her long red hair. She must be real, though, must she not, else whence comes this image of her in my head? Could it come of itself? Impossible! It must be some shadow of an actual girl with such length of thigh and flash of eye and smoothness of flesh and fiery pennant of hair, for I have no power of invention to paint her for myself. Nor is it a memory, for I have never seen the like or near it, nor any women indeed but my own mother, whose dear skin is like a prune and hair like wire. She must be real, then—and, being real, must be somewhere near, else why should her shadow tease and tangle me so?"

When he opened his eyes he saw a wet girl on the riverbank wringing out her long red hair, and he did not know whether

"And good morrow to you, sweet lad. Kathleen is my name."

the dream had brought her or she had brought the dream, and he didn't care.

"Good morning to you," he said. "I am Carth of the Cove."

"And good morrow to you, sweet lad. Kathleen is my name. My father is Houlihan, of whom you may have heard."

"Not I. I have heard of nothing and seen less. My mother keeps me close."

"Mother? Are you not too big now to be having a mother?"

"It would seem not. I surely have one. And she has me. She is a widow, you see, and childless save for me."

"What do you know of kissing and such?"

"Oh, she kisses me good-night every night. And upon my birthday, you know. A dry, flinching sort of business. Don't think much of it."

"Have you never been properly kissed by a girl?"

"You're the first girl I've ever met up close."

"Well, you have lots to learn and I have lots to teach, only I shall have to learn too while teaching. So let's be about it."

"Do you mean to commence now?"

"Now? Certainly now. In these matters it is always now. In fact, as I see you sitting up there sweet and savory as a roast piglet, I understand that all this should have happened before. I am fair famished for you, little pig. And ripe for marriage."

"But my mother has warned me about girls. I must not meet them, nor meeting, look, nor looking, speak, nor speaking, touch. I'm to avoid them altogether, the lovely, fresh, rain-smelling creatures. She will not have me marry until I am forty."

"Will she not?"

"She is most resolute. Promises to flay the skin off my backside if I do not heed her."

"And I promise worse if you do."

4

The Divided Husband

ome days later Finn was walking along a riv-
erbank, attended by cat and falcon, when a voice
screeched.

"Halt!"

It was a woman, standing on the road with wild hair and
flying shawls, her face lumpy and red as a fist. Finn stopped at
her word.

"Good day, mistress. May I serve you?"

"Have you seen a boy on your travels?"

"One or two. What class of boy would you be seeking?"

"An imbecile."

"I have met such indeed. What does your imbecile look
like?"

"Sweet, sweet, with angel-blue eyes and peach-bloom
cheek. Soft-spoken, gentle, all dewy with a mother's kisses."

"I do not believe I have met this lad. But I can understand
how you grieve to lose such a son."

"Lose him . . . lose him . . . I never did! He was stolen!"

"By whom?"

"I'm not sure. But my mother's heart tells me it was a girl

who came by water, the slut, to avoid my vigil. Came secretly, leering and fleering, to pounce on my lamb and carry him off."

And the woman danced in her rage, singing:

Calamity, disaster,
pestilence and plague.
I'll scarify and blast her,
break her head like an egg.

Then she turned to Finn and said:

"You are a doer of deeds, are you not, young sir?"

"I am, lady. Certain tasks claim my attention."

"And you are sworn to aid the weak and helpless, are you not?"

"I am."

"Then you must help me."

"Would you be describing yourself as weak and helpless?"

"Damn your eyes if I am not! I am a poor, lorn widow who has been cheated out of her only son by some sly vixen whom I will strangle with these two hands when I find her. You will help me, will you not?"

"In my opinion, widow, it will be your enemies who will be needing help."

"Oh, woe and wail away, how can I find them? They are fleet and I am slow. If I do not appeal to your chivalry, let me try your greed. For thirty years I have been skimping and scrimping, and now I have a pot of gold. A double handful of the lovely stuff do I offer if you help me find my boy."

"Keep your gold, lady. My deeds are not for sale. Nor am I free to refuse you however I may sympathize with your son and his abductress. I will help you find them. But once found, what follows is up to you. I will meddle no more."

"Just locate my Carth for me and I will do the rest and be grateful to you forever."

"Farewell, madame."

Not long after this the widow received a note from her son that read

Dear Mother:

You're wondering what happened to me. Well, it seems that I'm married to this girl who swam the river that morning and bade me be her husband. I told her you didn't mean me to get wed until I was forty, but she wouldn't listen. At first we were going to live in her father's barn, but after a few nights she decided that I wouldn't last very long if she took me home because he's very large and fierce and gets angry quite easily and has other peculiar ways. So we have set up housekeeping in a very comfortable hollow tree with a view of the river. Being a husband is very strange. But it's enjoyable too in its own way most of the time, and I'm doing quite well for a beginner, my wife says. Her name is Kathleen. Please come and visit us and stay as long as you like. Kathleen joins me in this invitation. She says no matter how bad you are her father is worse, and living with him has taught her to fear neither man, woman, beast, nor devil. Indeed it is true, she is very brave.

Love,
Carth

You can imagine how angry the widow was when she read this letter. She fumed and raged and stamped her foot and clawed the air and smashed a whole roomful of furniture before the red mist of her tantrum cleared and a little sense came back. She seized the note and went rampaging down the road until she found Finn's encampment.

"Good morning, widow," he said. "I did not expect to see you again so soon."

"Nor I you," she said. "Look at this."

*She seized the note and went
rampaging down the road . . .*

She thrust the note at him. He read it and smiled. "Well," he said. "This seems to let me off the hook."

"What hook? What hook? What do you mean *off*?"

"I mean I am no longer bound to find them. They have found themselves and told you where they are."

"You still must help me," she cried. "Don't you see this is a trap? She forced him to write this weasel-worded invitation. He never did it himself, poor, stupid, bullied darling. She made him write it, threatening some awful torment to his tender flesh. Now she awaits my coming with a meat cleaver up her sleeve and kettles full of poison brewing in case she gets to serve me tea. You must come with me and protect me against assassination like the young hero you are."

"Perhaps if you speak gently to your son's wife and do not accuse her of kidnapping the lad, and try to treat her as a human being instead of some wild beast—why then, perhaps, she in turn will hang up her meat cleaver and save her kettles of poison for another occasion. And you two will sit and drink tea and converse like two civilized creatures. Is that not possible?"

"Drink tea with that murdering slut, is it, in her hollow-tree den? Give myself into her treacherous hands completely? And never see light of day again? No, my fine Finn, you must keep your hero vows and come with me and help me thwart the plans of that red-headed young assassin, who has stolen away the innocent son and now wishes to rid herself of the poor grievin' mother."

"Well, there's no hope for it," said Finn. "I see I must accompany you on this charming visit. But I am not free until the day after the day after tomorrow."

"So be it," said the widow. "In two days' time you and I will go together to visit Kathleen ni Houlihan, and see what is to be done to save my boy."

But it was not yet to be. On the evening of that day a mighty storm struck the coast, one of the worst in memory, sending huge seas to drown the beaches, tossing boulders like pebbles, leveling whole forests. Nor did Finn have any way of knowing that this fearful weather was the opening salvo in the war between Vilemurk and Lyr.

In fact, Finn was comfortable enough in his cave and did not wholly regret the storm. "For," he thought to himself, "it may be that the hollow tree where dwelt the troublesome bride and groom has fallen in the wind as so many other trees have, and they have perhaps found another dwelling where the widow cannot find them. As for that harridan, who knows. Perhaps she was swept out to sea by a wave, or caught in the open and blown quite out of my life. Well, we'll just wait and see."

After the storm, Finn was left alone. His companions, the

cat and the hawk, had departed gleefully, for hunting is good in the aftermath of a storm. And the next day the widow appeared.

"Stir your stumps in there," she called. "Today is the day you keep your promise, Finn. We go a-visiting, you and I."

So it was that Finn, on that fair, cold blue-and-gold morning, found himself in the middle of a dreadful scene. For the raging widow hunted down the young couple. The hollow tree was gone; the forest itself was a tangled thicket of fallen timber where the great trees had been scythed down by the wind. But the woman let nothing discourage her. She followed her nose like a bloodhound, and led Finn straight to the bank of a river where stood the hull of a wrecked ship. Here Kathleen and her spouse had set up housekeeping.

There was no exchange of greetings. The widow let out a bloody howl and leaped right onto the ribbed hull of the ship, cocking her blackthorn cane to knock Kathleen's head off her shoulders. But the girl never flinched. Swift as a snake striking, she reached her long arm and twisted the stick out of the widow's clutch and broke it over her knee, then strode to the widow and stood facing her.

"Is this how you come a-calling, Mother dear? Were you never in all your long years taught manners, by any chance? Well, you've come to the right place to learn."

Finn and Carth stood horrified, watching the women. Mother and wife stood crouched, eye to eye, nose to nose, jawbone to jawbone, too close to shriek but berating each other in strangled whispers.

"He's mine, mine, mine, and you shan't have him!"

"He's mine now, and I shall keep him!"

"He has me, and needs no other!"

"He needs me, not his mother!"

Now the widow wound her claws into Kathleen's red hair and tried to pull it out by the roots. But the girl braced herself like a powerful white mare, stiffened the column of her neck, then snapped her head. The long red pelt of her hair snapped like a whip, lifting the widow off her feet and hurling her the length of the deck, where she fetched up against a rusty anchor. She rushed upon Kathleen, screaming:

"I'll tear the blue eyes out of your head, you wild hussy!"

"Come and try, Mother dear," crooned Kathleen, crouching, and rocking her long arms.

"Stir your stumps in there," she called.
"Today is the day you
keep your promise, Finn."

Now Carth of the Cove, who could not bear to see the two women in his life fight like this, rushed between them—unwisely, for each seized an arm and a leg and pulled at him, crying:

"He's mine, he's mine, he's mine!"

"Drop this wife, and come away with me, dearie," cried his mother, pulling with all her might.

"Cast off this mother and stay with me," said Kathleen, pulling with all her wondrous might.

Flesh and bone could not take this tugging. The boy came apart in their hands. Split right in two, he did, from crotch to pate. The mother was left holding half a son by arm and leg— one arm, one leg, one haunch, one shoulder, half a face split right up the bridge of the nose. And Kathleen, for her part, held half a husband, precisely the other half, and each half useless to mother and wife.

Finn, in a rage, leaped across the deck, seized the two halves of the boy from the women's hands, and laid them tenderly down, then clouted each warring woman along the side of the jaw, laying them out flat.

"Sure," he said, "you are the two shrews of the world and impossible for a man to deal with. Now look what you've done to this poor lad. Aye, and it shall be long work knitting him together, if indeed it can be done at all. For it takes much magic to restore a lad so split and torn."

He found a hole of the right size where a small tree had been uprooted, and stuck the widow in headfirst. It was a bit narrow, but he jammed her in till she fit snug, with only her feet sticking in the air.

"She's too tough to kill and too mean to die," said Finn to himself, "but this will cool her off a bit."

He began to look for another hole for Kathleen. But then he remembered suddenly the blue flame of her eyes, and the limber column of her neck, and her hair red as the oak leaf in autumn. And he returned to her and lifted her out of the wrecked ship and took her to the river where he laved her face until the cool water awakened her. She looked at him silently.

He said: "On second thought you shall journey with me to the far home of Angus Og, whose magic I will implore to rejoin the halves of your poor husband, whom you and your mother-in-law between you have succeeded in tearing apart. For it is a far journey I make and a great boon to ask at the end of it, and a heavyweight of dead body to carry in this sack, so I will not leave you here, but you shall come with me and help. It is your husband in the sack, after all."

"Who are you?" asked Kathleen. "And why do you thrust yourself into my household affairs?"

"I am Finn McCool. And I advise you to change your tone, my girl, or I may clout you on the other side of the jaw. For you are a beautiful creature to look at, but a terrible shrew. As for your household affairs, I wish I were heartily out of them. But I am under a hero vow to do favors when asked, and I was asked. And here I am. So shut you up, and come along."

5

The Captive God

That night, after their evening meal, as they sat on a bluff overlooking the sea upon which a path had been kindled by the moon, there was a rustling in the air, and a flash of green fire from four wild eyes, high and low, and Finn's companions, the hawk and cat, came to him from where they had been off hunting.

The falcon perched on Finn's shoulder. The cat, without hesitation, stepped into Kathleen's lap. And Finn noted with admiration that the girl was not at all frightened by the sudden apparition of the huge black tomcat with blazing eyes who shot out of the darkness at her. She stroked the cat, saying:

"Good evening to you, Master Puss. You're a handsome beast to be sure, but I see no one has taught you manners, leaping out of the black darkness like that."

She stroked his head and shoulders. He closed his eyes and purred his low, rasping purr. The falcon said to Finn:

"I have a tale for your ears. May I tell it now?"

"Tell away," said Finn.

"I speak too," said the cat.
"And in more cultivated accents . . . "

"Lord McCool, tell me: Did I hear that bird speaking to you and you answering it?" asked Kathleen.

"You did."

"Well, that's a marvel, now," said the girl.

"Not so marvelous," said the cat. "I speak too. And in more cultivated accents—without that hawky screech."

"You too!" cried Kathleen. "Well, I have been turned out of my peaceable home, and seem to find myself in the middle of an adventure, with strange companions. A meddlesome, gray-eyed stripling who calls himself hero and minds everyone's business for them, and claims an acquaintance with sorcerers and a hawk that speaks and a cat who boasts of even greater eloquence. Sure, and I've fallen into curious company."

"You've known worse," said Finn.

"May I tell my story?" asked the falcon. "I seem to have been interrupted."

"Proceed," said Finn.

"It's the kind of thing that interests you, Master. An adventure within an adventure, as it were. And all of it holding enough peril to suit even you."

"I'm listening," said Finn.

"I heard this story from a gull with whom I had been disputing property rights over the carcass of a fat fish, which he had caught, to be sure, but which I had made him drop. Anyway, he was a pleasant enough bird for a gull; we resolved our quarrel and got to be chatting of this and that. And he told me there was soon going to be a terrible fish shortage because of the anger of Lyr, God of the Sea.

" 'Why is he angry?' I asked the gull.

" 'You would be angry too, if you were a prisoner.'

" 'Lyr, a prisoner? But who can imprison a god?'

" 'Another god, of course,' said the gull."

And then the hawk told them what she had learned from the gull—a story that we already know. How Lyr wooed the ice maiden, of Vilemurk's wrath, and the vengeance he prepared. The rumor of the great crystal that had awakened Lyr's greed, and how the sea god had sped forth in his chariot drawn by flying fishes to challenge the Pig's Ploughman and all his dread company: serpent, frost giants, wind-master, and mist hags. And how he had flown straight into the Winter Fiend's ambush.

Such was the tale the hawk told Finn, sitting on his shoulder in a clearing of the wood, where the little fire Kathleen had cooked supper on made the tree shadows dance. But Finn and the tall girl sat motionless among the dancing shadows, still and rapt, drinking in the words of the strange tale told by the hawk.

"Go on," said Finn. "Don't stop now, just when Lyr is about to be trapped."

"Flying *fish*," hissed the falcon. "Imagine fish flying. Disgusting! Sure, and Lyr deserves what happened to him, employing such unnatural creatures."

The cat yawned in the firelight, half turning on Kathleen's lap, and lifted a paw to play with the plume of her hair.

"But what did happen to Lyr?" crooned Kathleen. "Don't leave us hangin', falcon dear. 'Tis a fearsome exciting tale, and you tell it so well. Did he fall into Vilemurk's trap, or what? Was he ambushed there in the northern wastes? Was there a battle, perhaps? Tell . . . tell . . ."

"Remember the big storm a few days back?" asked the hawk.

"Oh, yes," said Kathleen. "It fair leveled the forest over our heads. And didn't mighty waves pound the beaches, swallowing up fishing huts, sweeping away barns and byres, drowning cattle? Most terrible storm in years it was—and the next day my mother-in-law came a-callin'."

"Well, that big storm," said the hawk, "was only a tiny ripple of the tempest that raged when the forces of the Pig's Ploughman came raging out of ambush and fell upon the sea king."

"Go on. What happened?"

"I don't mean to leave you in suspense," said the hawk. "But unfortunately I cannot finish the story, because the gull never finished it. He got too hungry. The fish had been very scarce, and when he saw the shadow of a trout he dived at it, leaving me there. I waited for him, but he never came back. And I don't know how the battle ended."

No one said anything. Kathleen stared into the fire. The flames snapped. The cat yawned. Suddenly, across the orange face of the moon were pasted the black silhouettes of wild geese. A long flight of them, necks outthrust, wings low, honking faintly, almost a barking sound, like hounds of the air.

The hawk rose in the air and balanced herself just above Finn's head.

"Good night, all!" she cried. "I go a-hunting. We eat goose tomorrow."

She disappeared. The honking grew clamorous, alarmed, then nothing was heard save the snapping of the fire.

"What do you think, lad?" said Kathleen. "What happened out there in the northern wastes? How went the battle? Did Vilemurk conquer Lyr? Did Lyr prevail? Tell me your opinion."

Finn said nothing, but stared into the fire, gently biting his thumb.

"Don't sit there sucking at your thumb like an idiot child," cried Kathleen. "I asked you a question. I want an answer. I get excited by stories. I don't like them to stop before they end. And a good guess is better than nothing."

"You have no way of knowing," said Finn. "But I'll tell you now. I don't have to guess, because when I bite my thumb this way, the very one that was scorched when I fried the Wise Salmon—which is another story I may tell you sometime—why, then knowledge comes to me, and I know beyond guessing. I invoke this power only upon special occasions. Not for little secrets, you understand. But the fate of the sea god seems occasion enough. And as I bite my thumb this way, pictures appear in the fire, and I can see them."

"What do you see?" whispered Kathleen. "Tell me . . . tell me . . ."

"I see right into the awful depths of the earth that open out under the sea, void under void. I see beyond those depths into the central fires of the earth, where grows a pillar of rock, molten rock far under, then cooling, cooling, until finally cooled by the northern sea, where the rock turns into ice. From this granite

Finn said nothing, but stared into the fire.

base grows a mountain of ice, which is like a huge iceberg, but does not float. And beneath this mountain, right where the granite turns into ice, there to that massive shaft is chained Lyr, shackled by the heaviest bolts ever made by those twisted smiths who labor inside Vilemurk's smoky mountains and forge his weapons in the volcano fires."

"You see all that?" murmured Kathleen.

"Indeed I do."

"What else do you see?"

"Tilted in the flame I see the oceans of the world. They are lead colored now and have lost their shine. No fish leap, no gulls fly. Crabs and lobsters crawl out of the seven surfs, fleeing the beaches and trying to climb trees. Yes, there is grief upon the waters, for the god has fallen."

"Is he dead?"

"Gods cannot die. But they can suffer. And this one is suffering. Chained underneath, deprived of water and light and majesty—tormented by Vilemurk's bat-winged mist hags who gnaw at him with their snaggly teeth—aye, he suffers. And the waters grieve. And those who live off the bounty of the sea, sailors and fishermen and such, they will perish too."

"Terrible pictures you see there in the fire," said Kathleen.

"Yes, and I go to change them."

"What?"

"I go to free the God of the Sea."

"You? What can you do?"

"That's what I mean to find out. Farewell, I go north."

"And what am I to do, young sir, while you go cavorting off on your adventures? What am I to do with that bag of bones that was my husband? It's your fault I'm in such a plight. If you had not brought his mother to see me, I'd still be living happily with him on that wrecked ship. But no! You must try to act like a hero and meddle in my affairs, and bring that old witch raging down on us, so that the poor lad was torn apart."

"But I have promised to restore him," said Finn. "I deny that he was sundered by my doing; nevertheless, I have taken it upon myself to see him whole again. It is only by the mighty magic of Angus Og that his poor frame can be reknitted."

"Exactly," said Kathleen. "And you are supposed to be taking us to Angus Og. But now you abandon us. You choose to go waltzing off on some conceited errand to the northern wastes. I'll not have it! You must keep your promise to me, and leave the God of the Sea to those better able to conduct such high business."

"Will you be silent, woman?" cried Finn. "Buzz, buzz, buzz—I can't think! Nag, nag, nag—you drive me to distraction! Can't you see that I have no choice, despite my promise? I am shown a larger danger, and I must choose it. To challenge the Winter Fiend and rescue the sea god is a deed worthy of Cuchulain himself, best of the ancient heroes. It puts me in a fever to think of such opportunity. So you must wait. Your husband must wait. My promise must wait."

"Wait how long?"

"Till I return."

"And if you fail to return? If Vilemurk is powerful enough to capture the King of the Sea himself, what makes you think, puny mortal that you are, that he will not squash you like a bug?"

"Without peril there is no honor."

"And so, you will be destroyed. And I will wait here with my sack of bones through the long years until I grow old and gray and withered, unloving, unloved. No, thank you. I'm your responsibility now. You thrust yourself into my business and made it yours. I am not so easy to get rid of, you will find. Go north if you must, but I go with you."

"Kathleen, be reasonable. I have fighting to do. I'll have no time to take care of you."

"Perhaps I'll take care of you. I can fight too, you know. And pretty well . . . pretty well. So you may as well stop arguing.

You won't budge me. Where you go, I go, and that's that. As for this bag of bones that's my husband—well, we'll store it in a safe place and pick it up when we return, if we do. There's a good flat rock. We'll bury the bones under it, and they'll be safe from prowling dogs. Start digging, Finn. The moon grows pale and the waters grieve, and we have much to do, you and I.''

6

Fire and Ice

ith Lyr imprisoned and helpless, the Pig's Ploughman had his own way with the weather and clamped a weird frost upon Eire. Finn and Kathleen awoke to the coldest day in memory. The trees were clothed in ice, and a single sheet of ice stretched as far as the eye could see. A flight of wild geese froze solid in mid-flight and fell into the bay without losing its V-shape, making a great splash that froze into a net of ice.

Boy and girl were amazed but strangely joyful. Weak sunlight fractured off the icy trees in a dance of light. They saw fiery splinters of green, yellow, white, blue, paler blue, storm-pink lilac, and the purples of wrath; the crystal trees bore fire-fruit where the sun touched them. And bending in the wind and shaking their boughs, they made a tinkling ice-music for light to dance by.

That day which started so cold grew steadily colder, so cold that the sunset froze in the sky. Its weight overbalanced the horizon, and it slid down the tilted line of the sky to the North Pole, where it stuck, flashing there in a pageantry of frozen colors we call the northern lights.

Finn knew that this frozen sunset was of the utmost importance to him, but he didn't know why. He bit his thumb, muttering:

> Salmon, Salmon, I bite my thumb.
> Speak ye forth, be not dumb.
> Come to me this day of ice
> With fish-mouth words of wise advice.

As he spoke, the words themselves froze in the air and fell to earth, rearranging their letters and spelling out new words. This is what he read:

"Quickly! Visit the sunset before it slides away, and search its roots for the seeds of fire."

Finn bound long, straight branches to his feet like the runners of a sled. He slung his sword-belt to the falcon, who seized one end of it in her beak and drew Finn swiftly over the icy plain to the great frozen lake of flame. He felt small as a speck of dust, did Finn, when he came to the base of that pulsing, radiant wall of color. Cold light poured down, staining him with its rich dyes, and his blood sang at the loveliness. The falcon flew slowly, pulling him on his skis past arches and columns and ramparts of living color to the red roots of the sunset. He dug there with his knife and pried out the seeds of fire, white-hot little pearls of the primal flame that sprout with unbelievable speed when planted, and will nourish life or death according to the manner of their sowing, and must be handled only by heroes. He put them in his wallet and skied swiftly away as the sunset's weight began to tilt the horizon.

The vile weather held, shrinking the seas, stretching the polar ice cap. The north wind blew triumphantly, sweeping the warm sea southward and paving the path of its retreat with rock-hard ice tundra.

Vanquished Lyr, manacled hand and foot to the granite pillar of ice that supported the roof of the world, could not strug-

*He dug there with his knife and pried out
the seeds of fire, white-hot little pearls
of the primal flame . . .*

gle free. His oceans shrank, and fishermen and sailors perished.

It was only autumn, but the coldest autumn the island had ever known. The sun was all shriveled to a pinpoint of light, when it could be seen at all, but mostly it was not seen, for a queer, cold fog covered the shores, confusing day and night. As the month advanced, the cold rain turned to hailstones big as eggs that fell with such force as to kill cattle in the field. Men did not venture out unless they wore helmets. Their wives, when they left the house, wore iron pots on their head. Then, before October ended, the snow began to sift down out of the gray sky. And fell and fell and fell. No one knew what had happened to the weather, and why the Winter Fiend triumphed so and was able to torment these islands known as the jewels of the sea.

Only Finn knew, he and Kathleen. And they were far to the north, fighting through a giant blizzard. They were clad in white fur, which made them very difficult to see against the snow. Finn had gone hunting and had come back with a pair of huge polar-bear pelts, which Kathleen had cut and sewn into two mantles and two hoods for herself and Finn. These furs kept them warm in the teeth of the savage wind.

That night they held a council of war around their campfire.

Each night now he scraped off one of the pulsing golden pods, and that shaving was enough to start a fire anywhere—for it was a particle of the primal flame itself, which is at the center of all life and drops to us from the sun.

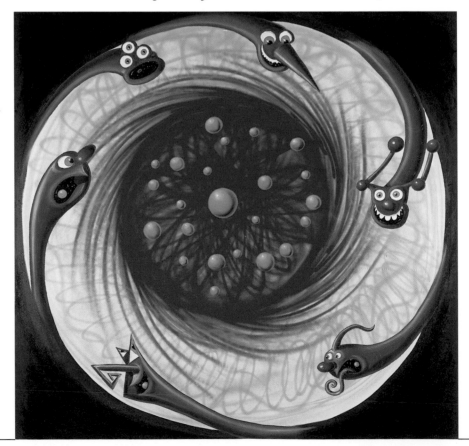

And how did they build a fire in a blizzard with no tree in sight, and no earth beneath their feet, only ice? Well, remember the seeds of fire that Finn had dug from the roots of the frozen sunset? Each night now he scraped a shaving off one of the pulsing, golden pods, and that shaving was enough to start a fire anywhere—for it was a particle of the primal flame itself, which is at the center of all life and drops to us from the sun. So each night Finn started a small blaze, which he fed with icicles, and the flame ate them as if they were twigs of wood, and leaped merrily, hissing and growing brighter as the snow fell upon it.

It was a wonder to the girl. She loved to watch the seeds sprouting into magic flame. She and Finn sat at the fire on this night, then, and plotted what to do. The hawk perched on Finn's shoulder, and the huge black tomcat lay in Kathleen's lap. And their fire was the only spot of light in all that howling waste.

"We've almost come to where I want to go," said Finn. "But what to do when we get there I do not know."

"That sounds like a song," said Kathleen. "A sad song."

"Yes, and I beg your pardon. A true hero should grow more joyful as the hour of peril approaches. But I am no true hero, you know."

"I didn't know. How could I tell? You're the only hero I've met, true or untrue."

"Well, take my word for it. By nature I'm a coward. I just pretend to be brave. And sometimes the pretense wears thin. I hate fighting. I can't bear the sight of blood. I don't even like loud noises."

"What in the world are we doing here then, picking a quarrel with the Winter Fiend himself and all his fearsome friends? Why must you pretend to be brave if you're really not?"

"It's a funny thing about courage. If you pretend hard enough it becomes real."

"Ridiculous! Why should you have to be a hero in the first place?"

"I didn't have much choice," said Finn gloomily. "My father was a hero. And various uncles. And grandfathers and great-grandfathers by the bushel, stretching back to the original family of giants who bullied their way onto this island and chased smaller folk off. I was the runt of the litter. Everyone was disappointed in me, and no one expected much in the way of sword-play and such. But, as it happened, I was even more contrary than I was cowardly. I decided to change myself, and went to work becoming what everyone expected me not to be. I have sought dreadful adventures and have come through with honor. But before every battle, I'm afraid. I'm afraid right now. But maybe I'll forget about it when the fighting starts."

"Are we close to fighting, then?"

"Close enough. See that giant pile of ice glimmering off yonder? That's the end of our journey. In the side of that ice mountain is the mouth of a cave. The cave winds down to the base of the mountain, which is the granite shaft to which Lyr is chained. The mouth of that cave is the doorway to our adventure."

"So you mean to go down there and rescue him," said Kathleen. "Is that it?"

"Ah, I wish it were as easily done as said. You see, I haven't told you about the dragon."

"What dragon?"

"The one that stands guard over Lyr."

"There's a dragon down there?"

"There is."

"That's all that's needed to make a bad case worse."

"Yes . . . "

"Actually, I don't really know what a dragon is. I've heard about them in the old tales, but I've never seen one."

"Well, those who have don't usually last long enough to tell about it."

"Are they that bad?"

"Imagine a lizard grown as large as a barn, with teeth the
size of plowshares, sharp as knives.
And great leathery wings to fly with."

"Worse. Imagine a lizard. You've seen a lizard, haven't you?"

"Yes. Nasty, scuttling, little reptiles with long tongues like springs that uncoil to catch bugs on the wing."

"Well," said Finn, "imagine a lizard grown as large as a barn, with teeth the size of plowshares, sharp as knives. And great leathery wings to fly with. All of him covered with leather scales so thick and tough he cannot be wounded by sword or spear wielded by the mightiest warrior. Now, this creature has a tail half the length of his body. This tail, when he lashes it, becomes an enormous flail. He can knock over houses with it.

Wreck ships. Beat a whole team of oxen flat and smash the wagon. And that's not all. Eight legs the beast has, each of them armed with a set of ripping talons. With a single swipe of his paw he can shred an oak tree."

"Any other features a girl should know about?"

"One more. And that, perhaps, is the worst. His breath. It is cold, deathly cold, colder than the essence of frost. When he breathes upon a living creature, its marrow freezes. It turns to ice. This particular dragon has been seen hunting walruses. He breathes their way, and petrifies them at a distance of half a mile. Turns them into blocks of ice, then ambles up to them and gobbles them down. That's the creature, my dear, who is guarding Lyr down in the cave."

"And you want to go down there and trick the dragon in some way and strike the manacles off the sea god? All by your little self? Confess—isn't that your clever plan?"

"I'm not exactly by myself," said Finn. "I have you, and you have been explaining to me for a thousand miles how dangerous you are when aroused. And I have my two trusted friends, the hawk and the cat. I have the sword given me by my father and the mission given me by fate."

"I still say it's a mismatch," said Kathleen.

"When mismatched," said Finn, "and that's the case usually with me, well, when facing up to a foe overwhelmingly strong, then, I've learned, you must use his own strength against him. That's the secret of winning against odds."

"What exactly do you propose?"

"I don't know exactly. That's why I'm discussing it with you. I'll tell you what there is of my plan, and invite your opinion."

"Thank you."

"Now it is clear," said Finn, "that we cannot possibly conquer the Winter Fiend. No, it takes a god to conquer another god. Therefore, what we must do is release Lyr so that he may use his power against Vilemurk."

"Release Lyr, is it? That's what I said you were after. I knew that before you started this heavy discussion. But how do you propose to do it?"

"Let's turn our mind to it," said Finn. "We know that Lyr is manacled to a massive pillar under earth, and that he is to be reached by entering the cave whose mouth opens out on that slope of ice mountain yonder. We also know that he is guarded by a dragon."

"It is that dragon that gives me such a poor opinion of our chances," said Kathleen. "You must admit you have painted a fearsome picture of the beast. All he has to do is breathe on us, and there we are, ice statues standing in a cave forever. And that's the best that can happen to us."

"We face a battle," said Finn. "And we have to know the worst so that we can do our best."

"I haven't had an easy life," said Kathleen. "But this worst is worse than any worst I've ever known."

"Well, now, the question is, what do we do?" said Finn.

" 'Tis the question indeed. I'm all agog waiting for your answer."

"We have discussed the dragon's powers," said Finn. "Now we must think about his appetites, for therein may lie a weakness. For instance, what does he eat, besides walruses, which are not his favorite food."

"I can just imagine," said Kathleen, shuddering. "He counts as delicacies, no doubt, lad and lass, cat and hawk."

"No doubt, but we'd make only a mouthful for him. He needs a more substantial dish. He eats seals by the hundreds. Hunts whale and octopus and giant turtle. As for land creatures, he prefers oxen and such huge viands. Here on the icy plains where game is hard to come by, his favorite meat is polar bear."

"Does he find them way down there at the bottom of the cave?" asked Kathleen.

"No," said Finn. "And you have put your finger on the very thing that may give us our chance. To hunt his food he must leave off guarding Lyr and climb to the mouth of the cave, and out upon the ice. There he lies in wait until he spots a polar bear, or a pair of them, and then he dines."

"Stop right there!" said Kathleen.

"What?"

"I'm beginning to get a glimmer of your idea, and I don't like it a bit."

"What don't you like?"

"What you're thinking."

"What am I thinking?"

"That you and I in our polar-bear cloaks and polar-bear hoods—why, we'd look like the dragon's favorite dish ourselves. Isn't that what you're thinking?"

"You're a clever girl."

"Not for long. Soon I'll be a dead girl if I don't look out. Dead and devoured and digested. Oh, why didn't I stay in my father's midden? Why did I have to leave the safety of that stinking barnyard and go husband hunting across the river? Now look at me: a thousand miles away from home, and freezing cold and widowed almost before I was wed, and about to become dragon fodder. Oh, woe and wail away!"

"Are you done with your lamenting?"

"Only for the moment."

"Well, do you want to hear the rest of my plan?"

"Might as well. Don't have anything better to do, and soon things will be much worse."

"Listen, then. In a few hours the dragon will get hungry. He will climb up out of his hole, up through the mountain, out the mouth of the cave, and onto the ice. And what will he see? Well, he will see two polar bears asleep. That's what he'll think he sees, for it is dark, and dragons are nearsighted anyway. So he'll come toward these two sleeping polar bears, who will be us, of course—and we shall be waiting for him."

"Without any eagerness whatsoever," said Kathleen. "Speaking for myself, that is."

"All right. He'll come up to the first one, who will be me, and open his great jaws and prepare to dine."

"Must you go into all this horrible detail?" cried Kathleen. "I get the picture."

"Not yet you don't. Look at this."

With a swift movement Finn shed his white cloak and hood, and stood in a black sealskin cape and cap. Kathleen could see only the glimmer of his eyes and the shine of his smile. When he tossed his mantle on the ice, why, it lay there plumply, looking for all the world like a polar bear.

"I've stuffed it with feathers," said Finn, "that the hawk has been collecting from every bird she strikes down and that I have been saving for this purpose. Look—does it not seem like a polar bear asleep?"

"Yes, it does. And that's about all I can say for it."

"The hide will hold not only feathers," said Finn. "When I finally doff it, it will hold something else, which the dragon will swallow down also. And that something else will be this."

He whipped something from his belt and held it toward Kathleen. She peered at it in the firelight.

"Your pouch—bearing the seeds of fire!" she cried.

"Exactly. That is what the dragon will swallow. And, perhaps, it will give him the biggest bellyache since bellies were made."

"What about the second sleeping polar bear?" asked Kathleen. "The one who's me. Or am I stuffed with feathers and fire too, and hiding in the shadows in a sealskin cape, which, by the way, you haven't given me."

"No," said Finn. "It will be you crouching in your white

Kathleen could only see the glimmer of his eyes . . .

cloak. And I have a special task for you. And the dragon will never reach you, if my plan works at all. Once he swallows the seeds of fire he should be very busy for a while. And I will deal with him, and try to direct his wrath for our own purpose. And you, you will slip into the mouth of the cave and descend to the depths of the cavern, taking my sword with you. There you will strike a blow for the shining waters of the world. You will raise my sword, which has been magically honed and can cut through any manacle—you shall wield my sword, you yourself, Kathleen ni Houlihan, too long a daughter, too soon a widow, you Kathleen, beautiful girl, brave and lovely one, who has chosen to leave the bag of bones that was her husband, and come adventuring with Finn McCool into this dire peril. Yes, you will use the sword that passed to me from my father, the great Cuhal, and you will strike the manacles off the God of the Sea, and release him to resume the war against the foul-weather fiend and his cohorts, who hold the sea in bondage and shrink the sun, and starve our folk. You shall do this and I do that. Between us—if fortune smiles, and we do not blacken her smile with our own fears—between us we shall conquer."

Kathleen stood tall. There was a deep throb in her voice as she said: "By the high gods, you can charm the birds off a tree, and a girl out of her judgment. I don't know if I'm brave or foolish, but I'm with you till the death."

"What do *I* do?" asked the hawk.

"I have a task for you. You must fly high and strike well to deal with the winged mist crones who will try to spread a fog about us and bewilder our enterprise."

"And I?" asked the cat.

"You will accompany Kathleen to the bottom of the cave, attending every step of her descent. You will need all your wits and claws and all the sorcerous tricks you learned from the witch who owned you to fight off the legions of frost demons that dwell in the cave and make a ferocious horde with their white leather wings and icicle teeth. Task enough for any tom."

"Until then I'll take a catnap. Wake me up when it's dragon time."

7

Dragon Time

Finn and Kathleen lay on the ice floe in their polar-bear capes. The uncanny night had fallen at noon, and a creeping mist had put out the few dim stars.

Kathleen tried to keep perfectly still, tried to clench her jaws to keep her teeth from chattering, but she was torn by fear. She began to cry, soundlessly, without sobbing. Her tears froze and fell tinkling on the ice.

"What's that?" whispered Finn.

"My tears falling. They're frozen, and chiming when they hit."

"Why are you crying?"

"From fear. Aren't you afraid? I thought you were such a coward. Why aren't you afraid?"

"I've been a coward for a long time. I know how to handle it. Now stop weeping. The dragon will grow suspicious. Sleeping bears don't chime."

Kathleen stopped crying and waited for the dragon to come. Now, Finn didn't want her to see the dragon coming. He thought that the sight of it might so terrify the girl that she would scream before it reached Finn, and that the monster would realize that it faced enemies and would blow its breath on them, freezing their marrow and turning them into solid lumps of meat to be devoured at his leisure. So Finn had warned Kathleen to keep her eyes down and not look up. But she found this very difficult. She heard a scraping, slithering sound, as if heavy chains were being dragged across the floe. She knew that the dragon was coming out of its cave and crossing the ice toward them.

She couldn't help herself. She had to raise her head and look. Then she wished she hadn't.

What she saw at first were two strange, smouldering pits, far apart, but level, growing brighter and redder as they came toward her. She couldn't imagine what they were. But then, as the chain dragging grew heavier until the very ice trembled beneath her, she realized that these pits of light were the dragon's eyes. By their light, she saw the whole terrible length of it—the huge jaws full of teeth, the ridged spine, the great spiked tail. She heard its claws now, scraping on the ice like enormous shovels, as the beast came closer and closer. Finally, she couldn't stand it any longer. She let her head fall into her hands again with a little moan.

Then she heard a loud, rasping snuffle which was its breathing, and she knew that the beast was almost upon them, coming to inspect the two sleeping shapes that were herself and Finn in their white fur mantles. She looked up again and, horror of horrors, saw the jaws gape and snap up the white heap that lay beside her. She couldn't believe that Finn would be quick enough to slip out of the bear hide, but he did. In the glare of the dragon's eyes she saw the black shape of Finn's body crossing her.

Then, an unbelievable roar, a mind-shattering rumbling, howling cry was torn from the dragon, who practically stood on its tail in agony. She didn't dare rise to her feet but simply curled herself into a ball and rolled away as fast as she could over the ice. She saw the dragon fall its full length, then scramble up and

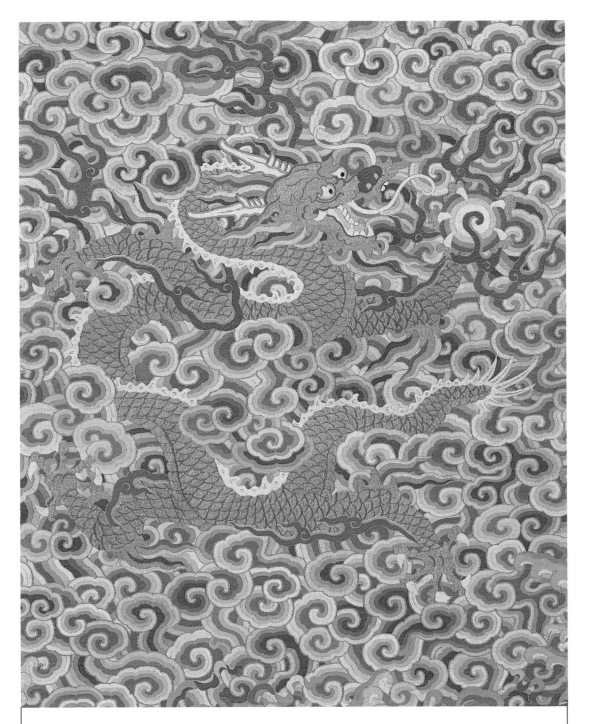

She saw the dragon . . . rise into the air
spouting flame like a volcano.

begin to beat its leathery wings with enormous force, and then rise into the air spouting flame like a volcano. And she knew the monster had swallowed the seeds of fire which were wrapped in the polar-bear skin, just as Finn had planned, and that there was a fire in its belly, and that it was in torment.

She watched in amazement as a huge gout of flame shot out of the dragon's maw and touched an iceberg, lighting up snow with radiant whiteness. She saw the iceberg hiss away in a giant plume of steam. She struggled to her feet again, peering about for Finn, but she didn't see him anywhere. The dragon bellowed again, and spouted flame. And by its light she saw an unbelievable sight: Finn riding the dragon's head, a dagger in each hand, stabbing the leather skull first on one side, then the other, trying to steer the monster in its flight. She understood what he was trying to do. Every time the dragon gushed flame the ice would melt and the sea would spring free. Finn, riding the dragon's head, trying to steer it by dagger thrust, was using the monster as a giant flamethrower to melt the ice by which Vilemurk had locked the seas.

"Oh, grief," said Kathleen to herself. "He's a dead man. How long will he be able to ride that fearsome head? He'll be burned alive, or shaken free and gobbled up by the dragon, or lashed by that terrible tail. Good-bye, Finn, unwilling hero, gray-eyed stripling of the golden tongue. Farewell, my boy."

But she had no time for mourning. Finn had told her what she must do. She picked up his sword, and made her way across the slushy ice to the mouth of the cave where Lyr lay bound.

Kathleen was right. Finn was in mortal danger. But he was in ecstasy, too. There was something about being perched high in the air on this brute head, steering the monster with daggers, and watching the great streamers of flame melt the icebergs and crack

the floes, and seeing the sea leap free—there was a glory about
this that dissolved his fears just as the ice was melted by the flame.
The great joy he knew then was a joy given very few to feel,
and those few are all heroes, of one kind or another. It was a joy

She watched in amazement as a huge gout of flame
shot out of the dragon's maw . . .
lighting up snow with
radiant whiteness.

that is felt when one turns a great key of nature—which is usually far beyond anyone's power—for Finn felt that he, actually, himself, by his own efforts, by his own wit and daring, was changing the weather, unlocking the sea, restoring the life of its creatures, and rescuing from starvation those who drew their bounty from the sea. And when a man or woman feels that joy in turning one of nature's stubborn keys, then he is apt to forget all lesser pain, forget his fears, doubts, hesitation. He knows the ecstasy of being a great natural force. The winds blow through him, he is warmed by the primal flame, and for a brief moment, before he flares into death, he knows that he has melted the icy indifference that reality turns to youthful hopes.

That is why Finn, who was no stranger to fear, as we know, kept riding the leather head, stabbing it this side and that with his daggers, steering the beast in its clumsy, leather-winged flight so that the flame of its breath played over iceberg and ice floe, vaporizing the massy piles of ice, splitting the floes, and letting the waters boil free.

So intoxicated was he with the joy of flight that he hardly realized when the dragon, growing more accustomed to the savage flame in its belly, became aware of the lesser torment on its head, and snapped its enormous length like a whip, sending Finn high into the air. The dragon then did a half somersault, pivoting upon its great wings, putting itself in position to lash out with its tail at the falling body.

Now the air was thick with the steam of melting icebergs, thick as soup. Finn saw the dragon turn and poise its tail, and he knew what the beast intended. Falling as he was, Finn doubled up his legs and kicked out with all his might like a bronco sunfishing, and was able to lodge himself in a thicker column of steam, which is what he wanted. It slowed his fall somewhat and partially hid him from the dragon. But the dragon struck too soon. The flailing tail missed Finn, but only by inches. He felt the point of its spike tear away his sealskin mantle, and the wind of the terrible lashing tail sent him blowing like a leaf, skittering sideways through the air. The force of it knocked him into a swoon. He fell onto a wedge of floating ice headfirst, and lay crumpled there, bleeding from the head.

8

Another Sword

e was plucked from the ice by a hungry mist crone whose favorite fare in all the world was human blood, especially hero's blood, drunk fresh from the skull. She stooped low, chittering, and plucked him from the floe and flew away toward her nest. But then she felt his heart beating and realized that he was alive.

"I'd better not eat him," she thought. "He's worth more than a meal or two. He's a well-made young lad, and will make a fine slave for the smith demons. For such a one, no doubt, they will trade me ten worn-out old slaves who, nevertheless, will furnish enough blood to last me through the season. Not hero's blood, to be sure, but we're in for a hungry winter, I know, what with Vilemurk's defeat. The master grows angry when the winter is warm, and the pickings will be lean, lean . . . ."

The mist crone bore Finn to the crater of a volcano in the dead middle of Vilemurk's secret domain. There she traded him for ten used-up smithy workers. Finn was taken down into the foul, smoky depths of the mountain, and the mist crone flew off, chittering happily, bearing a bladderful of fresh blood and a sack of fresh skulls.

The hollow mountain was a loathsome, sooty place, lit only by the volcano fire upon which the twisted smiths forge their weapons.

Finn awoke to find himself a slave in the smithy, which is one of the worst things that can happen to anyone. The hollow mountain was a loathsome, sooty place, lit only by the volcano fire upon which the twisted smiths forge their weapons. The slaves are used to tend the fires and work the bellows, and haul the ashes and scrub the anvil. They are kept half starved, allowed almost no rest, and are worked until they drop. No guard is kept upon them because they cannot possibly escape. Each one is chained by the ankle to a round, flat stone so heavy that the slave can barely trundle it along. Nevertheless, he is expected to keep up with his work. If he falls behind he is flogged almost to death. So the slaves drag their stones about from task to task as nimbly as they can. When completely worked out, they are either fed to the flames or sold to the mist crones, for the smith demons can always count upon a fresh supply of slaves. The Pig's Ploughman makes constant war on the other gods, and on humans, and is always taking prisoners. And prisoners of war were always enslaved.

At first Finn didn't care how soon he dropped from exhaustion and was fed to the flames. To labor ceaselessly in the strangling darkness, he thought, was worse than any death could be. He could hardly breathe, the air was so thick with charcoal dust and ash. And no matter how fast he worked he was beaten to make him work faster.

"Well," he thought to himself. "If it's time to go I'll take one or two of them with me. The next time anyone tries to beat me I'll snatch the whip from his hand and knock out his snaggly teeth with its butt, and wrap the lash around his neck and strangle him with it. Then the others will bash in my skull with their iron mallets and that will be that."

So he prepared for one last act of defiance, and immediate death. But then, for some reason or other, his wrath turned icy. His weird stubbornness arose, and his wits began to work.

"After all," he said to himself, "I've served an apprenticeship in suffering. I've been imprisoned before, beaten before, skillfully tortured. And didn't I learn endurance from ordeal, and the power of silence, and some of the arts of strategy? Am I to forget all that because of a few weeks' discomfort? No! Finn McCool does not surrender so quickly. He does not allow his enemies so easy a victory. His death will be dearly purchased.

Let me think now. Let me be true to myself and find a way out of all this misery, and pay back those who have made me suffer. That is the way of a man and a warrior."

So, instead of snatching his few poor rags of sleep that night, he lay there in grime and exhaustion, trying to make a plan. The next day at the forge he spoke to the head smith, who was just putting an edge to a splendid sword.

"Pardon, Master, but that blade looks dull."

"What!" cried the smith. "Miserable earthworm! How dare you address me without permission! How dare you pass an opinion on a weapon I have forged! What do you know of swords anyway, slave?"

"Like many a slave," said Finn, "I was a warrior once, and the son of warriors. I am Finn McCool. My father was the great Cuhal. His sword, by common admission, was the finest ever forged. That blade could shear off a bull's horns or a boar's tusks as if they were twigs. I have seen my father scythe down an oak tree as thick around as a span of oxen with one whisk of that sword. And I know for a fact, because the sword became mine after my father's death, that it could cut through any link of any chain ever made. It was this sword that cut away Lyr's shackles when he was Vilemurk's prisoner, and set him free to turn the tide against your lord in the recent war. For I, myself, gave that sword into the hands of the one who struck the chains off the sea god."

"That was your sword?" muttered the smith wonderingly. "Your very own, the blade of Cuhal? We knew, of course, that it must have been that blade that cut Lyr free, for no other could have done it. We forged the manacles right here in this workshop. As for the sword, I must tell you that it was made by my own father, who passed all his craft to me."

"If you're as good as your father," said Finn, "why can't you make a sword as good as the one he made for my father?"

"It was not made for your father," said the smith. "It was

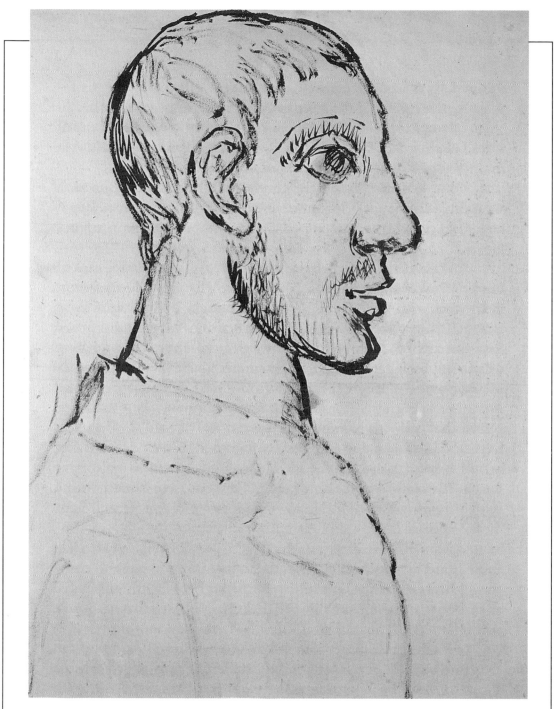

"If you're as good as your father," said Finn,
"why can't you make a sword as good as
the one he made for my father?"

king's own fountain. Each time he worked the molten ingot, shaping it into a murderous, elegant slenderness.

Finally, on the forge lay a tapering, two-edged blade, each of the edges honed razor sharp, and it came to a needle point. Before putting the final edge on it, however, the smith made its hilt. He twined leather strands about the rounded end of the blade. The leather had been cured from the hide of a newborn bull calf; it was soft and very tough. Then he inlaid the leather with delicately spun gold wire. This combination of bull-calf hide and gold filament made a supple handle that could fit itself to any grip, and would allow a warrior to keep his hold in the shock and ruck of the most violent battle.

The handguard was no simple crosspiece, but a deep cusp made of brass leaf, beaten thin as flower petals and welded together leaf upon leaf, making a guard that was as supple as leather and tough as steel. No blade could shear through it and wound the swordsman's hand.

Finally, just as night ended and the great gong sounded to call the slaves from their brief sleep, the smith honed the edge of the blade for the last time, wiped it down with an oily rag, and held it gleaming to the forge fire.

"Isn't it beautiful?" he said to Finn.

"Beautiful," said Finn. "As beautiful as the sword of Cuhal. But can it cut as well? We must try its edge."

"Here," said the smith, thrusting the sword into Finn's hand. "You try its edge. You will find it can cut this anvil in two. And when you have satisfied yourself that it equals or surpasses the sword of Cuhal and that I—I—am the author of this blade, why, then you will give it back to me and I will strike your head off your shoulders for your insolence."

"Well," said Finn. "I suppose it could be considered an honor to be decapitated by the best sword ever made—if such it is—but let me try it first before you finish your boast."

Finn made a pass or two in the air.

The sword maker heated the bar of metal red-hot . . .
shaping it into a murderous, elegant slenderness.

"Ah, nicely balanced," he said. "Now for the test."

But he did not strike at the anvil. He struck at his own ankle. As the smith stared in amazement, Finn struck off the chain which shackled him to the stone. He did a little dancing step and laughed into the smith's face.

"Why, nothing makes you feel as light-footed as being chained to a rock for a couple of months."

"What are you doing?" whispered the smith in horror.

"Testing your sword. Indeed, it is everything you claimed. It cut fairly through my chains. I wouldn't be surprised if it were good at heads, too."

Before the smith could take a step backward, the blade glittered in the forge light once again, and swept the troll's head off his shoulders. And Finn himself, moving swiftly and silently as the shadow of flame upon the rock wall, fled up the hills of slag, up, up, up, his feet spurning the ash and raising clouds of fine gray powder. Two sentries leaped to stop him. The blade flashed again, and two heads rolled in the ash. And Finn was out the mouth of the crater and rushing down the slope so swiftly he did not seem like a man at all, but like a goat leaping or a stone dropping.

Down the slope he rushed, down to the level ground, never breaking his stride. Onward he rushed, hurdling logs, leaping streams, into a girdle of trees. Through the trees, onto the beach. There, riding his luck—which is another name for hardship challenged and overcome—he spied a small skiff hidden in the reeds. It was a slender little coracle, made of hides stretched over wooden ribs, something like our canoe. He pushed it into the surf, jumped into it, and paddled away as swiftly as he could.

When he lost sight of land and knew that he was safe from pursuit, he stopped paddling, looked into the depths of the water and said: "O great Lyr, God of the Sea, you whom I rescued from captivity, O Lord of the Deep, I ask that you return favor for favor. Keep the sky clear and the waters calm, and send me a favoring wind that I may reach the shore of Eire. Any shore at all of the lovely land, I don't care. I'm no hard bargainer. Put me ashore at Leinster, Munster, Meath, or Connaught. I'll settle for any of them and walk the rest of the way, rejoicing. But let the winds be fair . . ."

The sea god answered.

MAN AND BEAST

9

How Lyr Paid His Debt

The sky darkened. Black clouds roiled up out of nowhere. Lightning stitched the sky. Thunder growled. The winds pounced from all directions at once, spinning the skiff crazily. Finn flailed with his paddle on both sides, struggling to keep the little boat from overturning.

Then the last of the sunlight was snuffed like a candle. A howling darkness fell. The skiff bucked like a wild horse. Finn felt himself going over. There was no way he could stop it. The coracle was turning turtle. He sucked in a deep breath before going underwater.

The water was cold . . . cold. He swam to the surface and immediately flung himself into the direction he guessed the boat to be. He grasped its slippery side, hugged it tight with such force he thought its wooden ribs would crack, but he didn't dare ease his grip. The wind was trying to pull him off. Struggling with all his might, he succeeded in inching his way up on the overturned skiff, and sat astride it, gripping it with his knees, clenching the keelson with his hands.

He had not lost his sword, though, nor did he have to hold on to it. It seemed to press its length against his leg like something alive. Its metal seemed to glow warmly there with some sleeping fire from its meteor birth. And it shone dimly, casting a small light so that he wasn't in utter darkness. When he grasped its hilt it was almost like grasping the hand of a friend. And, somehow, the dimly glowing, softly warming moon–metal sword kept him alive during that terrible night.

Dawn found him still clinging to the overturned skiff. Three-quarters drowned, punished by the wind, almost frozen— but still alive. The sun stood on the horizon like a battered tin dish, and the sea was lead colored. Then Finn saw the worst sight you can see upon the face of the waters: the long, sleek bodies of sharks turning all around his boat, showing their white bellies and their triple rows of teeth. They seemed in no hurry. They were trailing him, as if knowing there was no place he could go. But they came closer. There were seven of them, he saw, each one bigger than the next, and the smallest of them longer than his coracle.

"Looks like this is it, all right," said Finn to himself. "But I wish I knew what's up with Lyr. He's acting as if I were his worst enemy instead of the one who traveled so many freezing miles to unlock his domain from the grip of Vilemurk. If he takes notice of me at all, it's no friendly notice. For the sharks are subject to him, as are all creatures of the deep. And, sure, they mean me no good at all, and they're getting closer and closer. Well, I won't make it easy for them."

The sword leaped into his hand. As one shark turned within arm's reach just under the surface of the water, Finn struck him with a slashing downward blow and cut off the final length of him, as a fishmonger slashes the tail off a bluefish before he wraps it in paper to give to a housewife. Blood dyed the water. Finn saw the wounded shark disappear under the snout-faced rush of the other sharks who converged on him, burying him under their threshing bodies, and in the space of half a minute they had eaten him away to the bone.

"Wish I could say there was one less," thought Finn. "But there's a total of two more, because three new ones came to the feast."

He held his sword poised, but did not know which way to strike, for the sharks, with dreadful intelligence, were now ringing the overturned skiff, and coming at it from all sides so that if he struck in one direction, the rest would be upon him before he could strike the other way.

"You're lucky, my enemies!" shouted Finn. "The sharks are doing your job for you. And I shall never face you now, sword in hand. Farewell, enemies! Farewell, dear cat and hawk. Farewell, Kathleen, most curious girl. Farewell, Lyr, treacherous god. Farewell, Ploughman. And now a sharp farewell to you, my finny friends!"

Whirling the sword about his head, making himself a chaplet of blue fire for his final moments, Finn waited for the sharks to come.

Suddenly, they were gone. He heard an odd gobbling, clucking sound, and saw three enormous swans sailing across the water toward him. Huge birds, bigger than eagles they seemed, floating there. One swan rose upon its knuckled claws and stretched its neck and beat its wings, and, far away, Finn saw the last of the sharks slicing through the water. The sun was still tin colored and the sea lead colored, but where each swan floated was a pool of radiant blueness, as if the birds carried their own light.

"There's some magic at work," thought Finn.

He was surer of it still when he felt himself being lifted gently in the air and the skiff righting itself beneath him, and himself dropping back into it. The swan who had stood on its claws swam up to the boat. Its feathers flamed with such snowy brightness that Finn's eyes were dazzled, and he could not see. When his vision cleared, there was Kathleen seated in the coracle facing him. She wore a long, white, lacy dress that seemed to be

One swan rose upon its knuckled claws
and stretched its neck
and beat its wings . . .

spun of foam, and on her head she wore a crown of coral and pearl.

"We meet again," she said.

"Kathleen," whispered Finn. "You're more beautiful than ever."

"Easy now," said Kathleen. "Be very careful what you say. You're floating on Lyr's own sea, and there are things swimming about underneath us who can hear every word, and are sure to tattle."

"What are you talking about? Lovely Kathleen, I'm glad to see you. And you make less sense than ever. But thank you for chasing away the sharks—for it was you, I know. And why are you sometimes a swan now? Tell me all."

"Hush, then, and listen," said Kathleen. "Be doubly still so that you can hear me out and understand how our story ends. And also because that way you won't be uttering any dangerous words. I left you riding the dragon, and him spouting flame and melting all the icebergs. I never expected to see you again. But I did what you told me. I took your sword and crossed the melting ice and entered the cave, and went down, down through the dark passageway, down the center of the mountain, escorted by the tomcat who fought off the foul little trolls who serve Vilemurk down there. Down, down I went to where Lyr was chained to a great granite pillar. I lifted your sword and struck off the manacles. Just then the dragon must have passed directly overhead, and his flaming breath hit our ice mountain. All melted away in a cascading sheet of water. And Lyr, free again, floating on his own flood tide with the ice melting all about him, the sea rising higher and higher, Lyr was king again—free and regal, trident in his hand, spearing the mist crones and the frost legions, calling great blue whales from the deep who broached the surface of the sea, and fell with their tons of weight upon Vilemurk's minions.

"The battle didn't last long. Lyr rode the rising tide to victory. The ice was melted, and the seas were free again, and Lyr was king. I was swimming alongside him. Then I was riding his shoulder, clinging to his beard. And, well, he was in a happy mood and full of power and joy. And grateful to me, I suppose, for striking off his chains. Anyway, he took me to his castle at the bottom of the sea, and made me his wife. One of them, that is. But his favorite, I guess. Unless he's busier than even a god should be."

"So you're a queen now?"

"Yes, Finn, in a kind of strange, wet way, I'm a queen. Me. Kathleen ni Houlihan, daughter of my father who was lodged in his dung heap, stinking up the east wind as it blew across Leinster. Well, I have never forgotten my father. Indeed, he's an unforgettable kind of man. So I craved a boon of Lyr. He sent a finger of the sea curling inland, and its cleansing tide swept away my father's midden. And a green salt magic turned my father into the cleanest creature in the whole world of living things—a swan. There he is now, that swan. See how white his feathers are? You would never know that he was once the dirtiest widower in the history of grief, would you? And that he had built up a heap of regret around him that was the shame of the four counties.

When his vision cleared, there was Kathleen . . .

No, he's a swan now. A big, beautiful, royal swan. But he still has his angry red face. See?"

"And who's the other swan?"

"Why, bless you," said Kathleen. "That's my mother. For Lyr did me that favor, too. He called her back from the dead. Gods can do that, but they don't like to. Without that boon, though, the first one wouldn't have been any good, because my father would have refused to live as man or swan without his wife. There she is. Look at her. Isn't she beautiful? And this cleanliness now is no contradiction. For she was the cleanest little body anyone ever saw. So she comes rightfully by her feathers, and is very happy as a swan."

"Mother!" called Kathleen.

The smaller swan glided over to the boat.

"I want you to meet my friend Finn. It's him we owe everything to. He saved my life, you know, many times. And it was through him that I met Lyr. Greet him, Mother."

The swan spoke in a low, throbbing voice, very much like Kathleen's but gentler. "Greetings to you, Finn McCool. Thank you for all you have done for my daughter and my husband and me."

She folded her white wings around his neck and pecked him softly on the lips.

"Thank you, madame," said Finn, "for the sweetest kiss ever bestowed upon a shipwrecked man."

"No sweeter than you deserve, Finn, who have rescued me from the dead, and my husband from the filth of despair, and made my girl a queen."

She pecked him again on the lips. Finn heard a strangled gobbling and looked up. He saw the largest swan rising onto his knuckled claws in the water, and beating his wings and shaking his red wattles furiously, and stretching his neck, and hissing.

"You there," gargled the swan, who was Houlihan. "You there in the boat! What's that you're doin' with my wife? What's all this billin' and cooin'? What's the lout up to, darlin'? Is he trying to make free with you? I'll sink him so deep even the sharks won't find him."

He fluffed up his feathers so that he seemed to double in size, and swam slowly toward the skiff.

"Shut up, Dad," said Kathleen. "He's a friend of mine. And the best friend this family ever had. If it wasn't for him you'd still be on your dung heap, and I'd be long eaten by the dragon."

"Apologize to him, dear," said the mother swan. "Thank him for all he's done."

Houlihan clucked something unintelligible, and ducked his head underwater, pretending to feed.

"You're welcome, sir," said Finn.

The mother swan swam to her husband's side, and they both swam a distance away, and floated there, waiting for Kathleen. Finn said to her:

"What happened to Carth, who was your husband? Did you forget about him?"

"Oh, no," said Kathleen. "I worked a small magic there, too. He was too downy and gentle for a man, beaten too soft by his mother. So I changed him into an aspect of his true nature. He's a downy duckling now, and my pet. He swims about with me sometimes, and I fondle him, and feed him small fish, and he is very happy."

"And his mother?" asked Finn.

"I changed her according to her nature, too. She's a pelican now. It made little change in her appearance, actually. I just pulled out her jaw a bit, and bent her nose a little to meet it. And provided her with wings not unlike the sleeves of her dress. Her voice is the same. And she flies about, croaking raucously, diving for fish. What's more, just to prove I have a kind heart, I gave her a final gift. An egg that will never hatch—really a stone, you know, from the bottom of the sea, but shaped and colored like a pelican's

The mother swan swam to her husband's side,
and they both swam a distance away,
and floated there,
        waiting for Kathleen.

"The next time the gods fight, I'll stay neutral," said Finn.

egg. She can sit on it in her nest, and sit, and sit, and it will never hatch, never grow up, never fly away from its mother."

"Truly, you have a kind heart," said Finn. "And imagination to go along with it. I'm jealous of Lyr, Kathleen. I've never met a girl I fancied more."

"Hush now!" whispered Kathleen. "You fool! That's just the point. *He's* jealous of *you*. He knows our story. I told him the whole adventure, not realizing that his mood is of the sea itself. He's changeable as the sea, and as violent in his tantrums. He's conceived such an envy of you as to make your life unsafe whenever you venture near the water. I pray you, Finn, when you get back to shore, try to stay there. Dry land's the place for you, lad, because the sea god is not fond of you."

"The next time the gods fight, I'll stay neutral," said Finn. "You help one of them, and they both become your enemies."

And that's the end of this story. Kathleen changed back into a swan, and the three swans escorted the little coracle back to a shore of Eire, and Lyr did not strike again. But after that time, Finn was very careful whenever he found himself at sea.

Since that time, too, Kathleen ni Houlihan has figured in many legends. Sometimes she is said to be swan-born; sometimes she is known as the bride of the sea. Now we know why.

Since that time, also, dragons breathe fire.

Acknowledgments

Letter Cap Illustrations by Hrana Janto

Cover, WINTER KING *(1989) by Hrana Janto and William Giese, watercolor and pastel*
  Courtesy of the artists

Opposite page 1, TRACERY LIGHT WITH SUN, MOON, AND STARS *(ca. 1390), Austrian stained glass (15" × 15")*
  Courtesy of the Metropolitan Museum of Art, the Cloisters Collection, 1936 (36.39.2)

Page 2, PIG *(ca. 1988), Mexican mask, acrylic on papier-mâché (diam. 4")*
  Courtesy of a private collection

Page 4, *Tile from a mid-17th-century stove decorated with scenes from the Bible and panels representing the Virtues*
  Courtesy of the Metropolitan Museum of Art, Rogers Fund, 1906 (06.968.2)

Page 8, EVENING WALK *by Vincent van Gogh (1853–90), oil on canvas*
  Courtesy of the Museu de Arte, São-Paulo
    Photo: Giraudon/Art Resource, NY

Page 11, NEBUCHADNEZZAR *by William Blake (1757–1827), watercolor*
  Courtesy of the Tate Gallery, London
    Photo: Tate Gallery/Art Resource

Page 13, *Detail from* MIRAGE *by Mario Sironi (1885–1961), oil on canvas*
  Courtesy of the Gallery of Modern Art, Florence
    Photo: SEF/Art Resource, NY

Page 14, *Detail from* BATHER ON THE ROCKS *by Pierre-Auguste Renoir (1841–1919), oil on canvas*
Courtesy of the Duran-Ruel Collection, Paris
Photo: Scala/Art Resource, NY

Page 16, VISAGE MACULE DE ROUGE *by Jean Dubuffet (1901–85), oil on canvas*
Photo: Giraudon/Art Resource, NY

Page 20, A ROAD AT ST. REMY *(1890) by Vincent van Gogh, oil on canvas*
Courtesy of a private collection, Lausanne
Photo: Art Resource, NY

Page 23, A WINDISCH PEASANT WOMAN *by Albrecht Dürer (1471–1528), pen and ink on paper*
Courtesy of the British Museum, London
Photo: Art Resource, NY

Page 26, WINTER *(ca. 1770), one of four seasons from a set of ivory figures by Balthasar Permoser, hard-paste ceramic (h. 7 3/4")*
Courtesy of the Metropolitan Museum of Art, the Charles E. Sampson Memorial Fund, 1972 (1972.46)

Page 28, *Illustration from* A TREATISE ON SIAMESE CATS *(19th century), pen and ink on paper*
Courtesy of the National Museum, Bangkok
Photo: Luca Invernizzi Tettoni/Art Resource, NY

Page 32, SELF-PORTRAIT *by Abel de Pujol (1787–1861), oil on canvas*
Courtesy of the Musée des Beaux-Arts, Valenciennes
Photo: Giraudon/Art Resource, NY

Page 36, ORION IN DECEMBER *by Charles Burchfield (1893–1967), watercolor on paper (101.6 cm × 83.8 cm)*
Photo: Art Resource, NY

Page 39, FLAMING PEARL, *detail from emperor's 12-symbol dragon robe (18th century), blue silk twill with ornament, couched in wrapped-gold and -silver yarns (l., nape to hem, 56 5/8")*
Courtesy of the Metropolitan Museum of Art, Gift of Lewis Epstein, 1954 (54.14.2)

Page 40, HYPNOZEN *(1983) by Kenny Scharf, oil and spray paint on canvas*
Courtesy of the Smorgan Family Collection, Australia

Page 43, *A Chinese-style dragon (19th century), woodcut*
Photo: The Bettmann Archive, NY

Page 48, NUMBER 10, 1951 *by Jackson Pollock (1912–56), black ink and pen on paper*
Photo: Scala/Art Resource, NY

Page 50, DRAGON AND FLAMING PEARL, *detail from dragon robe worn by the Emperor or his immediate family (1862–74), satin embroidered in silks, seed pearls, coral; couched in gold and silver (35" × 55")*
Courtesy of the Metropolitan Museum of Art, Gift of Robert E. Tod, 1929 (29.36)

Page 53, DRAGON GRASPING FLAMING PEARL OF COSMIC KNOWLEDGE, *detail from Emperor's 12-symbol dragon robe (18th century), silk and wrapped-gold tapestry (l., nape to hem, 57")*
Courtesy of the Metropolitan Museum of Art, Rogers Fund, 1932 (32.23)

Page 55, SNOW AND FIRE *(1987) by Paul Georges, oil on canvas (40" × 60")*
Courtesy of the artist and Anne Plumb Fine Arts, NY

Page 58, *Treasures from the Tomb of Childeric (ca. 5th century), Merovingian art*
Courtesy of the Musée des Beaux-Arts, Troyes
Photo: Giraudon/Art Resource, NY

Page 60, MEN AROUND A FIRE *(1989) by Earl Staley, acrylic on canvas (72 1/2" × 96 1/4")*
Courtesy of the artist

Page 63, SELF-PORTRAIT *(1907) by Pablo Picasso (1881–1973), pen and ink on paper*
Courtesy of the Gallery of Twentieth-Century Art, Berlin
Photo: SEF/Art Resource, NY

Page 67, *Detail from* CLANDESTINE BULLET FOUNDRY *by Francisco Goya (1746–1828), oil on canvas*
Courtesy of the Palacio Real, Madrid
Photo: Scala/Art Resource, NY

Page 70, MAN AND BEAST *(1969) by Neil Jenney, oil on canvas (61" × 58 1/2")*
Courtesy of the artist and Vivian Horan Fine Art, NY

Page 74, SWAN, *detail from* THE VISITATION, *fol. 38v,* TRÈS RICHES HEURES DU DUC DE BERRY *(1375–1425), watercolors and gilt on parchment*
Courtesy of the Musée Conde, Chantilly
Photo: Giraudon/Art Resource

Page 76, STUDY FOR SCHEHERAZADE *by René Magritte (1898–1967), gouache on paper*
    Photo: Charly Herscovici/Art Resource, NY

Page 79, *Plate from the* SWAN SERVICE *(ca. 1737–41), German Meissen hard-paste ceramic (h. 2 1/4" dia. 13 1/4")*
    Courtesy of the Metropolitan Museum of Art, Gift of Rosenberg and Steilbel, Inc., 1958 (48.165)

Page 80, A WISE MAN *by Paul Klee (1879–1940), oil and gouache (25" × 26 1/2")*
    Courtesy of a private collection, Bern
        Photo: Giraudon/Art Resource, NY

BOOKS BY BERNARD EVSLIN

Merchants of Venus
Heroes, Gods and Monsters of the Greek Myths
Greeks Bearing Gifts: The Epics of Achilles and Ulysses
The Dolphin Rider
Gods, Demigods and Demons
The Green Hero
Heraclea
Signs & Wonders: Tales of the Old Testament
Hercules
Jason and the Argonauts